Sports Stars

JIM McMAHON

The Zany Quarterback

You should know one thing about Chicago Bear quarterback Jim McMahon. He is different. He does crazy things. He is zany.

He does things his way. And, usually, he does them well.

Most football quarterbacks don't like getting hit. Not by bigger, stronger defensive linemen.

Jim talks with the Bears' head coach, Mike Ditka.

Jim says he doesn't mind. Most quarterbacks follow instructions from their coaches. But Jim will change plays at the line of scrimmage. Sometimes he doesn't think the play sent in will work. So he changes it.

"Jim thinks he's the best passer, the best runner, the best blocker on the team," says Bear head coach Mike Ditka. "A lot of players wouldn't do what he does."

He is different. And he is not afraid of pain.

One thing Jim does worries Ditka. That is when Jim tries to run with the ball when he can't find an open receiver.

When Jim can't find a receiver, he runs. He tries to get a first down.

"Football is a physical game," Jim explains. "I don't mind getting hit. You're going to get hit anyway standing in the pocket. When I take off for a first down, I'm not trying to be a hero. I'm just trying to get the first down."

"Jim always wants to be one of the guys," says teammate Keith Van Horne. He is an offensive tackle for the Bears. "He likes to get down in the trenches with us, get dirty, get turf burns. He wants marks all over his helmet."

Jim left his mark of Super Bowl XX. He completed 12 of 20 passes for 256 yards. The Bears beat the New England Patriots 46 to 10.

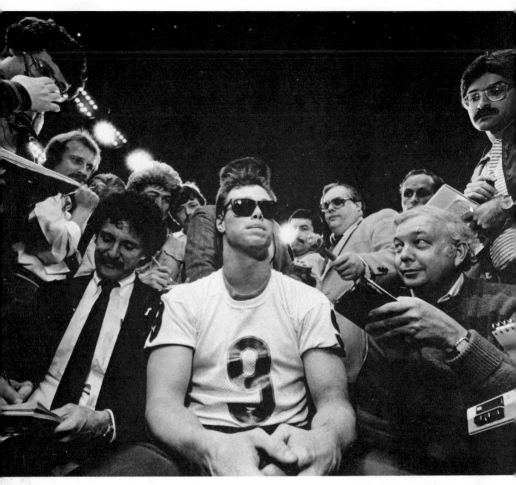

Reporters swarmed around Jim after the Bears won Super Bowl XX. The lights from the TV are very bright, so Jim wore sunglasses.

When the game was over, Jim met newspaper reporters in the locker room. He was wearing sunglasses. Some people thought he was just trying to be different. But he has a reason.

Jim has to wear sunglasses. When he was six years old he had an accident. Jim and his brother were playing cowboys and Indians. Jim had a knot in the leather string that tied his holster to his leg. He wanted to untie the knot. It was hard to do. So he tried using a fork.

"So I'm trying to get the knot out," he said, "And, wham!"

The fork jumped from the knot. It stabbed Jim in the right eye. Jim spent the next two weeks in the hospital.

"The doctors thought I might have severed the retina," Jim said. The retina is a delicate part of the eye. It turned out the retina was all right. But the eye is still damaged. It is unable to adjust to bright light. It means Jim must wear sunglasses whenever it is bright.

Jim was a natural athlete as a child.

"Since Little League, everything's always come naturally to me," he says. "I don't really have to think too hard about what's going on. It's just a God-given talent, I guess."

Jim's accident did not hurt his vision.

As a boy, Jim's idol was former New York Jet quarterback Joe Namath. "Joe played hurt a lot," says Jim. "And when he said he was going to do something, he did it."

Jim also looked up to former Minnesota quarterback Fran Tarkenton. He liked former Washington quarterback Sonny Jurgensen, too.

Jim played football in high school. He also played baseball and basketball. In a state tournament baseball game, he once hit a bases-loaded home run. It tied the game in the ninth inning. In basketball, he stole an inbound pass.

The Dallas Cowboys sack Jim.

Then he scored with five seconds remaining, when his team was trailing by a point.

His family moved from San Jose, California before Jim's sophomore year. They moved to Roy, Utah. Before the football season started, he had beaten out two older quarterbacks. He won the starting job.

After high school Jim wanted to go to Notre Dame University. He wanted to play quarterback for the Fighting Irish. They are one of the most popular college teams in the nation. But Notre Dame wasn't very interested in him.

Jim can change plays if he feels it is necessary.

So Jim settled on Brigham Young University in his home state of Utah. It turned out to be a wise decision. Brigham Young's coaches liked to pass the ball a lot. Jim fit right into their offense.

In fact, Jim did well at Brigham Young. He set or tied 71 college passing and total offense records.

Jim never liked to lose. In the 1980 Holiday Bowl, Brigham Young trailed by 20 points. They were playing Southern Methodist University. There were a little over four minutes left in the game. Brigham Young coach LeVell Edwards wanted to punt the ball. Jim talked him out of it.

Then he threw three touchdown passes. Brigham Young won 46 to 45.

"I don't think those kinds of situations are tough as far as pressure is concerned," Jim said later. "You're not out of a game until it's over. You have to make your breaks. When you do get your breaks, you have to capitalize on them."

"There was never any doubt in my mind about Jim," said coach Edwards. "Physically, he has the tools to do it. He has an accurate arm and he's mobile. Mentally, he knows how to read defenses. But more than that with him are the intangibles. Jim has a way of making great plays out of disastrous situations."

"Jim is a guy who's going to take some team to the Super Bowl someday," Edwards said.

And that's what the Chicago Bears were hoping. They made Jim their first-round pick in the 1982 National Football League college draft. The draft lets each pro team take turns selecting players who have just finished college.

The Bears found out right away how different Jim was. "He's not like most quarterbacks," said Bear head coach Mike Ditka. "He probably is most unlike any quarterback in the league. You tell him to go bang, bang, bang and he goes bang, boom, boom!"

Walter Payton, Jim McMahon, Matt Suhey, and Keith Van Horne

Some people said Jim should spend more time studying film of the other team's defenses. Ditka said it wasn't necessary.

"That doesn't mean he isn't more into the game than any other quarterback," Ditka said. "Some guys look at film over and over. I think Jim looks at it once, and then he starts thinking. He sees it in his head more than he would see it on a screen. He sees situations flash, and then he says, 'If this happens, I go this way.'"

Ditka played tight end with the Bears in the 1960s. He admires some of Jim's habits off the field. "Every quarterback I ever knew hung around with his receivers," Ditka said. "This guy hangs around with his linemen."

Jim is serious about the game of football.

"That's just Jim's nature," said teammate and close friend Ken Margerum. "If you just look at the way he acts, you'd think the guy's crazy and undisciplined. But when it comes down to his business, he's real serious."

And Jim's business with the Bears was football. The United Press International wire service voted him the National Football Conference Rookie-of-the-Year in 1982. In 1983 he set three Bear passing records.

But he had some bad injuries in 1984. Playing against the Los Angeles Raiders, Jim suffered a lacerated kidney. It forced him to miss the last six regular season games and the NFC championship game. The Bears lost 23 to 0 to the 49ers in San Francisco.

In 1985, Jim's goal was to make it through the season without an injury. It was not to be.

Meanwhile his reputation for being zany continued to grow. In summer training camp, he tried to cut his own hair. He did a very poor job of it. So he asked teammate Willie Gault to help. Gault only made it worse. Jim ended up with a Mohawk haircut. Then he decided to shave his head completely.

Jim's hair started to grow back. He didn't look like a quarterback. He looked more like a punk rock singing star. But this didn't bother him a bit.

Early in the 1985 season, Jim hurt his back and leg. He wasn't able to start in the third game against the Minnesota Vikings on national television. Steve Fuller started in his place.

The Bears were behind 17 to 9 in the third quarter. Jim talked Ditka into letting him go into the game.

On his first play, Jim avoided a Minnesota blitz. He threw a 70-yard touchdown pass to Gault. Then the Bears got the ball again. Jim threw a 25-yard touchdown pass to Dennis McKinnon on the first play. On the sixth play of the next series, Jim threw a 43-yard touchdown pass to McKinnon.

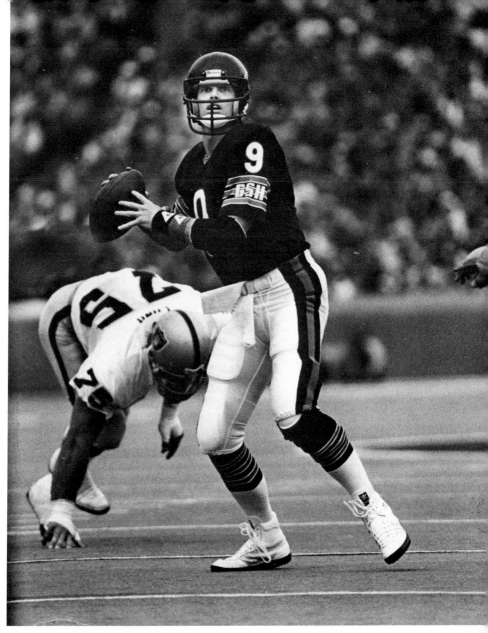

Jim looks to see if his receiver is free.

Suddenly the Bears were ahead 30 to 17. Jim had thrown three touchdown passes in less than seven minutes. That's what he did in college in the Holiday Bowl. The Bears won 33 to 24.

Many experts said this was the turning point in the Bear season. And it didn't end until they had won the Super Bowl.

"When Jim's in the game, we're a different ballclub," McKinnon said.

Every Thursday night during the season, Jim would join his offensive linemen for dinner. It gave Jim a chance to spend some time with the guys. He really admires them. Jim is only 6 feet

Behind Jim, left to right, are Keith Van Horne, Kyle Clifton of the New York Jets, Matt Suhey, and Jay Hilgenberg.

1 inch, 190 pounds. But, he said, "Heck, if I was 6 feet 4 and 280, I'd be a lineman. I could have a good time doing that."

Someone asked Bear center Jay Hilgenberg to imagine Jim as an offensive lineman. "He'd be a tough pulling guard," Hilgenberg said. "And he would definitely be wearing black, high-topped shoes."

The week before Super Bowl XX in New Orleans, there were many reports. People thought Jim might not be able to play. He had sore muscles in his lower back. But Gault had a Japanese friend who specialized in acupuncture.

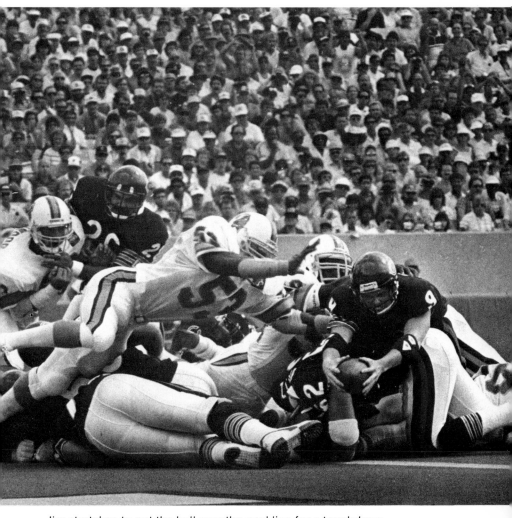

Jim stretches to put the ball over the goal line for a touchdown.

Acupuncture is a medical science popular in Japan. The doctors place tiny needles to relieve pressure in injured areas.

Gault and Jim talked to the acupuncturist. They arranged for him to fly to New Orleans. Then he treated Jim. It paid off. By game time Jim was fine. And his confidence had rubbed off on his teammates and coaches.

It was like Super Bowl III. Joe Namath, Jim's idol, was the Jets quarterback. The Colts were heavily favored. But Joe said his team would beat the Colts. Most people thought Joe was out of his mind. But the Jets *did* beat the Colts, 16 to 7.

Jim just misses getting sacked.

"Jim reminds me of Namath," said Bear defensive coach Buddy Ryan. "Even if the defense didn't play great, you knew the guy could get hot and get you back into the game."

"Jim McMahon's strength is turning bad plays into big plays." said San Francisco coach Bill Walsh. He added that Jim's arm is probably stronger than 49ers quarterback Joe Montana's.

The Bears played the Patriots in Super Bowl XX. Both the defense and the offense played well. Jim completed 12 of 20 passes for 256 yards. He also ran for two touchdowns. *Sport* magazine picked teammate Richard Dent as the

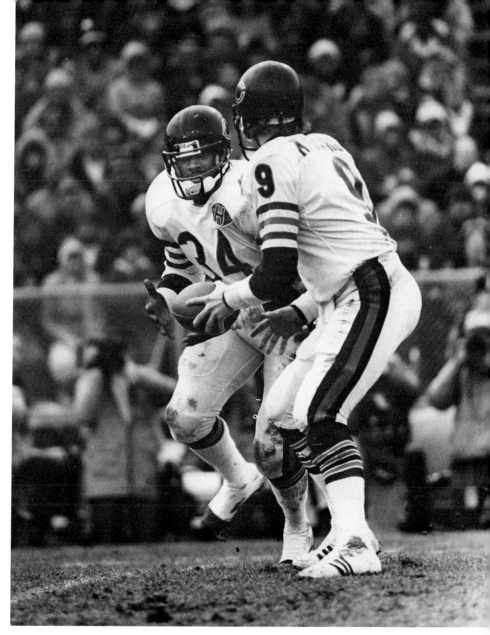

Jim hands the ball off to Walter Payton.

Most Valuable Player of the game. But Jim finished second in the balloting.

"Jim's not what people think about as a pro quarterback when they're growing up," Hilgenberg said.

Near the end of the season, Jim wore a headband with the name of a sports equipment company on it. NFL Commissioner Pete Rozelle said that was against the rules. He fined Jim $5,000.

During the playoffs, Jim teased Commissioner Rozelle. He wore a headband with Rozelle's name on it.

Rozelle could only laugh at the headband with his name on it. He later praised Jim for

Pete Roselle's name is on Jim's headband.

wearing headbands during the Super Bowl. The headbands brought national attention to at least two worthy causes.

When it was all over, Jim was happy to return home. He could spend time with his wife and their two daughters.

Jim is a good quarterback. He is different. He is zany. But as a father, Jim is no different than most.

CHRONOLOGY

1959—Jim McMahon is born on August 21 in Jersey City, New Jersey.

1965—Accidentally Jim sticks a fork in his right eye. It limits his ability to block out brightness. That is why he wears sunglasses.

1981—Jim finishes his college career, setting 71 NCAA Division I passing and total offense records at Brigham Young University.

1982—The Chicago Bears make Jim their first pick in the annual NFL draft.

—Jim finishes his rookie season with the Bears with what is believed to be the highest quarterback rating (80.1) for a rookie in the history of the league.

1984—On November 4, Jim suffers a lacerated kidney playing against the Los Angeles Raiders. The injury forces him to miss the rest of the season.

1985—On September 19 in Minneapolis, Jim shakes off a back and leg injury. He comes off the bench to throw three touchdown passes in less than seven minutes to lead the Bears to a come-from-behind 33 to 24 win over the Vikings.

1986—Jim completes 12 of 20 passes for 256 yards and runs for two touchdowns in the Bears' 46 to 10 victory over the Patriots in Super Bowl XX.

ABOUT THE AUTHOR

Brian Hewitt is a sportswriter for *The Chicago Sun-Times*. He covers the Chicago Bears and the rest of the NFL for his paper.

He has covered six Super Bowls and writes for a variety of national magazines. He also has written a book about Bear defensive tackle William Perry, entitled *The Refrigerator and the Monsters of the Midway*.

Mr. Hewitt recently won a national writing award from the Professional Football Writers of America for an article on Bear running back Walter Payton.